Into the Wild Blue Yonder

A Play by Carl Nelson

i

DEDICATION

To anyone who loves the ins and outs of conversation and the characters who produce it. Here are my attempts to pen a satisfactory one.

Plays by Carl Nelson:
Into the Wild Blue Yonder
Personal Growth Through Copier Sales
Ollie's Day Out

Essays by Carl Nelson:
The Audience is a Mob

Poetry by Carl Nelson:
A Poet's Past Lives
Shoving My Way Into the Conversation

All are currently available through Amazon books.

CONTENTS

ACKNOWLEDGMENTS

Into the Wild Blue Yonder was first produced as a Showcase Production at ArtsWest in West Seattle in September of 2001. Thom Sweeney Directed. Steven Loch played Dr. Perhl. Eric Morgan played Claude. Robert Myers played Bert. JC McClure played Bernice. Marissa Febus played Jackie. Troy McVicker played Herb/Flight Officer. And Voices of Ensemble played Fifi. Dramaturg was Nadine Trenton. Suffering Wife was Lynn Nelson.

INTO THE WILD BLUE YONDER

CHARACTERS:

Claude Gustafson
Dr. Pehrl: Claude's Swiss (Jungian) analyst with thick accent
Bert Gustafson: Claude's older brother, businessman
Jacqueline (Jackie) Meyers-Gustafson: Bert's sexy, blonde, second wife.
Bernice Gustafson: Claude and Bert's mom
Herb Bottleman: airport acquaintance of Bernice's
Fifi: cream-colored, stuffed Chihauhau
Handsome WWII Flight Officer: to stick head out at curtain call

INTO THE WILD BLUE YONDER

ACT ONE

"...opera in particular is an imitation of human willfulness;" Auden

PRIOR to the curtain opening, music from Carmen, 'L'amour est un oiseau rebelle' by Bizet as sung by Teresa Berganza, soprano, begins. The opening predatory string work of this melody will foreshadow BERNICE's appearance and turns of mind throughout the play, just as musical phrases of other types (such as the theme song for "Frasier" opening the scenes in DR. PEHRL's office, various renditions of "Amazing Grace" to introduce the funeral parlor set, plus "I'll Fly Away" and bubbly mystical music to mark BERNICE's descents and ascents) will foreshadow the appearance and turns of other scenes.

SETTING (as produced): The stage is partitioned into several sets by placement of the furniture. Center stage are two overstuffed chairs representing the Gustafson library-den. Outlining this set stage rear is a fireplace mantle with implements and family pictures (backstage right), and a tall leafy plant and wet bar (backstage left). Downstage right is a overstuffed leather chair with an end table facing a violin- shaped psychiatrist's couch center stage right. This area represents the psychiatrist's office during DR. PERHL's sessions. At other times it will be absorbed into the activities in the library-den of the Gustafson home. The area stage left is cleared for the dancing which takes place in Act One. In Act Two, stage left will be the funeral parlor with coffin and chairs. (The two center stage overstuffed chairs will have been carted offstage.) Center stage back is a half- flight of steps between the parted curtains on which the angel BERNICE will descend and ascend.
As the scene begins, CLAUDE and BERT are occupying center stage.

left,   (Music fades as DR. PERHL rises from out of his office chair, downstage to address the audience. He is dressed professionally but with tasteful flamboyance; his vest has stars and comets. He sports wire-rimmed glasses.)

SCENE 1

(DR. PERHL in spotlight)

DR. PERHL: Good evening. This evening I want to talk to you of a special patient of mine, a Mr. Claude Gustafson. (points out CLAUDE) Who has involved me in this fantastic story - which otherwise, couldn't be more normal! Which is as follows, more or less in the order of its psychological unfolding.

But first. Everybody who comes in here wonders, "Dr. Perhl, what should I do this?" And, "Dr. Perhl, what should I do that?" And who really figures out anything, for certain, ever? Nobody! Believe me! I am a psychological analyst!

So second, I want to make it plain all what I think. So that you will know what is going on! for goodness sakes. You paid good money.
        (a beat)
I think that Life is just one big Journey in the Dark. And that to help us along we must find, manufacture, or COERCE a little Romance. For heaven's sake! all of us fighting both tooth and claw for this same thing ...just a little hug.
        (a beat)
And so it goes with my patient Claude, moving timidly - like a rag picker, you bet! picking his way through the peoples battling it out...
        (points to CLAUDE)
like "one, lone voice crying in the wilderness!"

(spotlight changes to CLAUDE)

CLAUDE: (loudly, circling) I tell you Bert, our mother is a stalker.

BERT: (more loudly, evading CLAUDE) That's right Frank. I want you to sell two thousand shares of the Ebcon.

CLAUDE: Bert. I think that you should take just a few minutes to listen to me because, I've been getting reports from the retirement villa where mother stays. And they say she has been causing trouble among the male occupants. Because apparently she pursues them up and down the halls and follows them into the activity areas and bothers them in their rooms, and generally harasses anybody with a... (raises finger) ...penis!

BERT: Excuse me Frank. (covers phone.) CLAUDE.

CLAUDE: There's something I need to talk to you about Bert. Something we need

2

to discuss.

BERT: Frank? Listen. Can I get back to you? We're having a dinner party here for my mother. Yes. She's going to be 85 in a couple days. Sure, I'll wish her well.
        (puts away phone)
What is it?

CLAUDE: I believe mom invited this older man here tonight because she is thinking about marrying him.

BERT: What older man?

CLAUDE: The one who's already HERE. He's in the house!

BERT: Claude. Maybe you should just mind your own business for at least several hours each day. You would be surprised how your personal interests can grow and accumulate.
        (taking messages from his phone)

CLAUDE: Well I'm alarmed. Because I see an aspect of our mother's personality surfacing whose presence I have predicted either silently, or at the top of my lungs! for over... (checks watch, as he sees BERT check his watch again) twenty years at least. I tried to warn dad. I tried to warn you. I tried to warn MOM. And all to no avail. Everybody has called me crazy, or most commonly just haven't wanted to deal with it, because they figured it just involved me and the circumlocutions... the ravings of an inadequate persona - which I will admit to.
        (a beat)
But nevertheless, I am afraid what we are about to witness is the eruption of our mother's truest, and most primitive SELF; a kind of atavistic coming of age! A fierce, savage, Something! A wild, raw, rude, protean, preliterate Something! I feel, I have INTUITED since childhood - like a great reptile whose tail slams the bars - but whose apparent nature has yet to break the surface.
        (a beat)
And now, frankly, I'm alarmed.

BERT: (snapping phone shut) Little brother? When I'm not worrying about mother, it seems I have to worry about you. Because on those few days when mother is not driving me out of my mind, you are there to tell me she should be.
Now just settle down. You're too excitable. You get yourself worked up over nothing. I swear, one little flutter of the curtain in the moonlight...
        (Music from Carmen begins again.)
...and you always rose up from the top bunk as if you'd seen a ghost.

BERNICE (very nervous, and tentative, enters)
>> (BERNICE is an eighty-five year old woman with a beehive hairdo, who
>> is made up like an Italian streetwalker with padded breasts.)

CLAUDE & BERT: (turn, scream)

BERNICE: (screams)

BERNICE: (collecting herself) For Pete's sake! I wish you wouldn't do that.
>> (CLAUDE circles like a nervous stray cat.)
Get over here. Now! I want you to return grace tonight at dinner. I want you to do
the blessing.

CLAUDE: I'll pray for you, mom.

BERNICE: I do not need your prayers. (inhales) I'm in the trim of health.

CLAUDE: Nothing is too difficult for prayer mom. Troubles, sickness, neurosis, (quotes
Blake) "the mind's forged manacles".
>> (mimics hairdo with hand gestures to BERT while mouthing
>> the words, "What's with the hair?")

BERNICE: Maybe you had better just thank the Lord you're alive! And do what I
say. (uneasy, to them both) Now listen up. And don't get cute. We have a guest
already here! tonight, and his name is Herb!
Herbert! Bottleman. He got bumped off his flight at the airport due to thunderstorm
activity, and it was a real Godsend! that I happened to be there also - and didn't look
like hell, (she wiggles) to boot - so that I could offer him a good hot meal within
the bosom of our family.
He's downstairs right now.

CLAUDE: You want me to welcome Herbert into our family? Into your bosom?

BERT: Who is this Bottleman?

BERNICE: No!. For heaven's sakes, no! He is a complete stranger and has yet to even pop
the question.

>> (a beat)

BERNICE: You say grace. Now if that's too much to ask, just tell me.

CLAUDE: I would love to return grace mom.

BERNICE: How gracious of you.

(a beat, as BERT tests her coiffure)
What? Is there something wrong with my hair?

BERT: No! It's been beaten to quite stiff peaks.

BERNICE: (to both) Fine. Stand up straight then. And quit slouching!
        (BERNICE hands CLAUDE a feather duster)
And here. And... YOU.
        (BERT jumps.)
You're not wearing a tie.

        (Lights off.)

BERNICE's harsh voice: Go put on a tie!

SCENE 2

SETTING: DR. PEHRL's office, which exists in a small lit area of the GUSTAFSON den, downstage right, consisting of his wing-backed leather arm chair with end table and a leather analyst's couch. DR. PERHL is sitting in his leather chair listening, with his notebook and pen lying on the end table. CLAUDE is lying on the violin neck shaped leather analyst's couch in the fetal position.

CLAUDE: And so my brother never listens. My mother never listens. Even this Herb Bottleman, who I haven't even met yet - I will go as far as to predict - will already! be into the loop far enough, I predict! ...not to listen.

DR. PEHRL: (sad eyes, listening) So... "The world is too much with you, late and soon."

CLAUDE: Boy. Yes. (surprised) That's poetry...

DR. PEHRL: (points to bookcase) That's Wordsworth! And he believes you...! And I believe you. You may not know this, but this is the reason most people come here.

CLAUDE: For poetry?

DR. PERHL: Yes, and no.

CLAUDE: It's not because they are nuts?

DR. PEHRL: No. You have been squeezed out of the footlights. That is all.

>   (a beat)

DR. PEHRL: Do you think you are crazy?

CLAUDE: No. But am I a good judge? Both Bert and Mom think that my bubble isn't in the middle. That the cheese has fallen off my cracker. That I'm not the sharpest knife in the drawer. And look at me! ....I'm seeking a second opinion.

DR. PEHRL: Ha, ha. The cheeze on the cracker... (taking notes) ...arrow to.. falling off... (to CLAUDE) That's a good one.
>   (a beat)
Mister Gustafson. Might I call you Claude?
>   (CLAUDE nods)
Most of the people I see - who make up my practice - have nothing organically wrong mit zer (taps head) ...noodle.

CLAUDE: (apprehensive) Am I one of these?

DR. PERHL: Oh ja.

CLAUDE: (relieved) Then why am I here?

DR. PEHRL: What have you just toldt me? Why would anyone listen to you, when you won't listen to yourself? You silly nut.
>   (smiles)
I like you already!

CLAUDE: Huh?

DR. PERHL: That, basically, is what our job is to find out!

CLAUDE: Why people won't listen to me, or why I won't listen to myself?

DR. PERHL: All of the above! Plus,
>   (a beat)

...think of it as an 'introductory offer' or perhaps 'a Blue Light Special'. But I would venture also, that you are bothered by... your mother.

CLAUDE: That's true!

DR. PERHL: That she frustrates you! And makes you angry.

CLAUDE: (recoiling, nervous) Wow, that's so true.

    (a beat)

This is an odd business.

    (DR. PERHL leaning back, lighting pipe, puffing)

DR. PEHRL : (pointing at CLAUDE with his pipe) Not so odd a business, I think, as the mind!
    (a beat)
Or any mind, that is. With lurking desires, like so many crocodiles drowsing in the brackish, sappy green waters of the Unconscious... like so many innocent, harmless logs floating in the sun!

    (lights off)

SCENE 3

SETTING: Light on in the GUSTAFSON library-den.

CLAUDE: (with feather duster, mulling DR. PERHL's remembered words)
Alright, maybe, I'm... evil. But still! at heart, every creature must feel good about themselves, or.. or why would they go to all the bother to exist?
    (BERT enters wearing tie, and rubber gloves with pail   and toilet scrub
        brush in hand.)

BERT: Good question. I snuck up on her for a little affection - just to deposit a little kiss!
    (BERT holds up toilet scrubber.)

and she's got me.

CLAUDE: You tried to kiss mom?

BERT: I was just trying to be on my best behavior because of an ongoing conversation I have had with Jackie. So I went up to mother to tell her how much I am going to try and make this evening work for her because of how much we are, well, (struggles) ... FOND... of her, and mom said, "Well I'll be darned Bert. That's great! Because do I have just! the job for you."

BERNICE: (sticking head in) Bert!

BERT: Mom?

BERNICE: You didn't do the toilet bowl! Now go back and do the bowl!

BERT: But the maid has done! the bowl.

(BERNICE enters pulling a vacuum.)

CLAUDE: (trying to be nice) You want me to vacuum?

BERNICE: (stuffing vacuum behind another door) No, it's too late to be thinking of vacuuming, for Pete's sake.

CLAUDE: Mom, when you get mad, it just depresses me.

BERNICE: (applying makeup before mirror) What is it? Did you say something? How do I look?

CLAUDE: You look busy.

BERNICE: (in a dither) I try to stay active.

CLAUDE: (circling, getting in BERNICE's way) You know ...

BERNICE: For heaven's sake! What is it?

CLAUDE: I think that all this furious activity of yours may actually represent... an avoidance of death.

(toilet flushes, and BERT enters carrying toilet scrubber, pail)

BERNICE: (looking in mirror) For Pete's sake. ...If you don't kill me first.

CLAUDE: (wringing hands) I didn't say that I wanted to kill you mom.

BERNICE: (to BERT) And you?

BERT: (waving toilet brush) No! Not me.

BERNICE: (nodding) You both just want me to slow down somewhat ...so death can come and get me.

CLAUDE: That's not what we mean at all.

BERNICE: Then, what is it that you mean?

CLAUDE: What we are trying to say is that sometimes a person... Who. Is. Going. at a Slower Pace. Sometimes reaps a greater appreciation of life. Because they have a chance to smell the roses.

BERNICE: Claude. I have slowed down enough to smell enough roses. What I am trying to do now is to speed up!
        (Snapping cosmetic case, as we hear HERB enter.)
...because I smell a man.

        (Enter HERB BOTTLEMAN, a short, bent, bandy-legged
                codger leaning on a cane, wearing a checkered sports coat
and   bow tie, with flaring eyebrows and wide hips.)

BERNICE: Herb! I am sorry. My sons and I found that we had more to talk about than we had anticipated. I hope that you haven't felt abandoned?

        (JACKIE enters carrying FIFI)

HERB: (taking JACKIE's arm) Abandoned? No! In fact, I feel like a tiger. Recharged! I feel reborn. And with this rebirth, I feel, an awakening! Is more like it. Yes. That's what it is.

JACKIE: (breathy, blonde, resplendent) Herbert and I have found an affinity. Herb has a very open mind. We have been discussing all sorts of things. I am a Gemini, Bert. Did you know. that? While Herb is a Taurus! Ooh!

FIFI: yips and panting

HERB: My toes! are tingling.

JACKIE: And I've enjoyed myself a lot too.

HERB: Jackie is short for (with French accent) "Jacqueline!"

JACKIE: Herb finds me interesting. What do you think of that, Bert?

>   (BERT - caught with toiletbrush and pail - doesn't look like   he
>   thinks very much of it.)

HERB: She wears a perfume with a haunting bouquet. It makes my head ring. I've
had to adjust my earpiece twice already. Such is her effect upon a man.
>   (to BERT)
How do you stand it?

BERT: Maybe you'd better sit down, Herb.

BERNICE: Why don't you sit down here with me, Herb?

HERB: Why?

BERNICE: (roughly) I want to tell you my Zodiac Sign!

>   (HERB and BERNICE struggle as BERNICE propels HERB
>   towards the couch.)

>   (BERT, JACKIE and CLAUDE move away.)

>   (Pizzicato sounds of an opera love aria begin, as HERB and
>   BERNICE sit, side by side, on the couch.)

HERB: (disheveled, looking around for JACKIE) Bernice? What's the big
idea?

BERNICE: Herb. You aren't old, and you are very spry. But you need your rest. You
need to learn to sit.

HERB: I know how to sit. It's getting up! that I'm going to have the devil of a time
doing now.

BERNICE: Then just stay put. So we can talk.

HERB: But I don't want to talk!

BERNICE: Then, just listen.

HERB: (scanning for JACKIE) I don't think I'm even made to listen.

BERNICE: (looking violent) Herb, take a breath!

HERB: (with puffed cheeks) ...What for?

BERNICE: Because I have a confession.

HERB: (rising) I don't care what you've done.

BERNICE: It's not! that kind of a confession.
    (a beat)
And you're my guest. So just squat.

HERB: Bernice, I'm a free agent. I'm a free man.

BERNICE: You're a free roaming rooster is what you are! And we all know just the remedy for that...

HERB: (protecting genitals, drops cane)

BERNICE: (warmly) ...is marriage.

HERB: (leaning away) Ah. Er, Bernice? Would you mind if I got up to take a little tiddle?

    (HERB wriggles, and grabs for cane.)

    (Spot shifts to BERT and CLAUDE and JACKIE, who are peeking in.)

CLAUDE: I don't believe this. Since age ten! I have been saying to anyone who would listen that there was something terribly wrong with our family. Dad never spoke - and look at what it's gotten me! Everybody thinks I'm insane, except! I am happy to say, a professional psychiatrist.
    (sees BERT and JACKIE's look)
Well... what of it?

BERT: What are you talking about?

CLAUDE: And who tried to warn you all? Who said, "Our mother is possessed by the Negative Mother Archetype, as symbolized by the Russian Bear! And that it most probably stemmed from a childhood inability to incorporate HER OWN OVERWHELMING MOTHER - a bewildering, cyclonic presence such as we all witnessed in grandma - into her own nascent ego?"

BERT: (to JACKIE) That's almost exactly! as he began to sound by age ten.

JACKIE: (blinking) What did he say? ...Your dad NEVER spoke?

BERT: He wasn't allotted much time.

CLAUDE: What could he say? "Help! I am being held hostage by the Negative Mother Complex?"
(spotlight expands)

BERNICE: (looks around) (sighs). Well, anyway.

CLAUDE: (hoisting large cake, leading others) Happy birthday, mom!

BERNICE: What?

ALL: Happy Birthday!!

(Toilet flushes. Sound of door opening and shutting.)

BERNICE: Oh? OH!!

ALL: (begin to sing Happy Birthday, but not enough to owe royalties!)

(CLAUDE, carrying the large cake, leads them all offstage into the dining room.)

HERB: (reappears, looks around) Auuhhh?

(lights out)

SCENE 4

SETTING: Post dinner, in the Gustafson den.

JACKIE: Herbert. It certainly was a pleasure speaking with you over dinner. Until you arrived, I had known nothing about estate planning, annuities, or debentures.

HERB: The pleasure was all mine! A stock's value is the product of a company's real worth divided by the total number of common shares minus outstanding debts and held bonds.
         (BERT enters with coffee.)
Whereas futures! are determined by the increment of rise and fall in the values of (gazing at her butt) speculative issues! Asset allocations, you see. It's nothing.

JACKIE: (taking coffee from BERT) My shy husband keeps all these thoughts to himself.

HERB: Say, you're quite a looker! This is good coffee, too.

JACKIE: Thank you!

BERNICE: (entering) Herb. I made the coffee.

HERB: No kidding.

JACKIE: Bernice made the coffee and nearly the meal besides. She's a driven woman. I've tried to slow her down but it's like standing in front of a moving train.

HERB: I know what you mean.

BERNICE: (to JACKIE) Some men like a woman who is capable and industrious and isn't afraid of work.

HERB: (straightening bow tie) There's some things that catch a man's eye, that's for sure.

BERNICE: And YOUTH is all a state of mind, I believe. Marriage isn't just a province of the young. It's all a matter of how young you feel.

HERB: That's it! (perspiring from closeness to JACKIE)
Younger women, you know. Feel I'm hearing that tremendous roar of the ocean. Feel

like I'm hearing my youth shouting back at me, over the years.

BERT: (raising voice above the ocean) That would be from quite a distance!

HERB: That's what I'm saying! She makes me kind of fluctuate, you know?

BERNICE: And ability and strength of character will stand out!

HERB: (to audience) And tits! Big tits will surely grab a man's eye.

    (a beat)

    (Spotlight moves towards CLAUDE who has pulled
    BERNICE to the side., while HERB is busy trying to insinuate
    himself between JACKIE and BERT.)

CLAUDE: Mom. Sometimes men don't like to be pursued.

BERNICE: And what do you know?

CLAUDE: Well, I imagine....

BERNICE: That's right. You imagine! And if I don't pursue a man, how in the world am I going to catch one? Am I supposed to just IMAGINE one?

CLAUDE: Usually mom, it's the men who pursue the women. They seem to feel more comfortable doing that.

BERNICE: That's all fine and good Claude. But then, if nothing happens, what would you propose that a woman do? That she just sit?

CLAUDE: I suppose that she would try to look more attractive. To change how she appears, or even ...appear human?

BERNICE: Change, change, change. Why should I change? And what if that STILL doesn't work? Or that she happens to attract the wrong sort?

CLAUDE: I'm not an expert. But do you really think that Herb is the right sort?

BERNICE: He's alive, isn't he? He's still kicking?

CLAUDE: (motioning to HERB pursuing JACKIE) Yes, but...

BERNICE: You are so conservative! I am the elderly person here. Whatever happened to the sexual revolution, and women's liberation? Where have you been son? The rules are all different nowadays! My goodness, wake up! In fact, it's one of the few benefits I can see to having lived so long. A woman used to have to wait around like an idiot! just twiddling her thumbs, HOPING that the right man might come around... might FIND his way to the door. And now, we can just go out and grab one as easily as men pick up a six pack at the corner store.

CLAUDE: It's not a matter of being conservative, mother.

BERNICE: Oh, you are the most hesitant person around.

CLAUDE: That's because I have found life to be very unscrupulous and unforgiving, and the complexities immense!

BERNICE: (moving off) All the more reason to just barge forward, I say.

        (a beat)

BERNICE: (claps) That's it! Dance with me Herb.

CLAUDE: (calling) We all have emotional needs mom!

BERNICE: (to HERB) I do not have emotional needs!
        (separating HERB and JACKIE)
Let's show these youngsters how it's done.
        (BERNICE puts on music: "Little Brown Jug" by the Glenn Miller Orchestra)

        (HERB is reluctant to leave JACKIE)

BERT: Forget it mom. I say we just drive the old relic somewhere, remove his dental plates and leave him.

HERB: That boy of yours? (stepping out) He has a mouth on him.

        (BERNICE and HERB trottle out.)

        (They dance.)

JACKIE: (to BERT) That was cruel.

BERT: (calling out) I'm not sure our Homeowner's covers this!

BERNICE: (swaying) They say you can tell a lot about how two people would be in an impending marriage by the way they dance.

HERB: Bernice, you're overwhelming!

BERNICE:: Thank you Herb.

HERB: (head in her breasts) I mean it! I can't breathe.

BERT: (to JACKIE) How much longer are we going to have to witness this?

JACKIE : (to BERT, swaying) It wouldn't hurt you to learn to dance, and to become a little more romantic.

BERT: (calling out) Try to keep your zipper up Herb!

JACKIE: (calling) I hope that when I'm seventy-nine years old Herb! and Bert is gone, that I can meet a man like you!

HERB: (calling to JACKIE) Why wait?
        (showing off)
(to JACKIE) Hey there! Bodacious. You're a dish!

BERT: (shouting) She's my wife!

HERB: (shouting back) Well... What a waste!

BERNICE: Herb! (breathing hard.) Control yourself!

JACKIE : (to BERT) You see? Even strangers! pick up on our emotional estrangement.

CLAUDE: (waving vials) Do you want your heart medicines mom?

BERNICE: No!

HERB: (dancing) Hey there, Cupcakes! I practice free love. How about casual sex?

BERNICE: Oh no you don't!

HERB: (pulling) Quit Bernice. Quit! I'm a free man! ...I'm a free agent!

BERNICE: (breathing harder) Oh no you're not. You're MY guest!
        (a beat)
And Bert? As far as I'm concerned, that Jackie of yours is just a gold-digger and a little tramp!

HERB: (lunges for JACKIE.) That's how I like 'em!

BERT: (in HERB's path) Why you lecherous old fart.

JACKIE: Are you going to fight? Bert?

BERT: We'll see.

BERNICE : Herbert! (holding HERB back) Stifle!

JACKIE: For me? Bert?

BERT: I said, we'll see!

        (CLAUDE grabs the fireplace implements and clangs them.)

CLAUDE: Could we all just stop a minute to look at what's happening here, rationally?

        (HERB and BERNICE are going around in circles.)

BERT: This old crate is trying to steal my wife! That's what's happening!

HERB: (adjusting hearing aid) I heard that!

BERT: I said it loud as I could!

JACKIE : (standing alone, completely isolated) Help me, Bert. Fight for me, Bert. (waving fists) ...Fight!

BERT: ?

        (HERB struggling.)

BERNICE: Herb! Quit!

CLAUDE: Mom? It doesn't appear to me like Mr. Bottleman... that is, Herb! here is looking for marriage.

BERNICE: (thrashing HERB) Oh Claude. Men don't know what they want!

(BERNICE falters, falls.)

CLAUDE: MOM!!!

BERNICE: (convulses) (death rattle)

HERB: (turning) Oh what is it now, Bernice?

(BERNICE is dead. ALL are gathered around in shock.)

(BERT dials 911 on cellular phone)

SCENE 5

SETTING: Funeral parlor with whiskey bottle perched on coffin. The song "Amazing Grace" is heard. We hear JACKIE's Chihuahua, FIFI, bark offstage, and BERT howl. Bert has been drinking. We hear the sound of FIFI panting.

BERT: That's it. Come on now. Do your thing.

(Sounds of FIFI peeing.)

CLAUDE: (offstage voice) Bert, I believe that you could have urged FIFI a little bit further than the front stoop!

BERT: (Sounds of BERT peeing.) It's the Call of the unfettered Wild!
(BERT howls like basset hound.)
Got to do our thing! Well, Fifi. Time for corpse watching.
(BERT re-enters dragging FIFI, with sounds of FIFI panting.)

(CLAUDE enters after.)

FIFI: (barks upwards)

BERT: What is it girl?

(Mystical bubbly music, as...)
(BERNICE descends from the ceiling and lands with a resounding thud!)
(BERNICE is dressed entirely in beige with tiny pair of wings.)

BERNICE: (excited, with arms open)

BERT: (screams)

BERNICE: Claude?

CLAUDE: (screams)

BERNICE: (disappointed) Don't get so excited boys. It's only your mother. You've known me for years.

BERT: (poking corpse while looking at BERNICE) Mom?!

BERNICE: (upbeat) I hear you've been saying some nice things about me, Bert.

BERT: I've been trying mom.

CLAUDE: There IS life after death.

BERNICE: Oh, it's much better than just breathing the air again, son. It's more like doing cartwheels and forward flips!

CLAUDE: (circling) And you've got wings!

BERNICE: (turning, embarassed about how tiny her wings are) Yes, I do.

FIFI: (excited yipping)

BERNICE: What's that?

BERT: It's Fifi, mom.

FIFI: (more yips)

BERNICE: I take it you're still married, Bert.

BERT: Like a rock, mom.

BERNICE (shutting the lid on FIFI and brightening) Anyway, about Heaven.

(Echoing sounds of FIFI yipping...)
From what I can see, the drinks are better, the jokes are better, the cars are all new, and they all live in grand palaces.

BERT: Palaces? (a beat) Everyone is RICH?

BERNICE: That's it. That's the story. Heaven is even something you could aspire to.

BERT: Mom. I HAVE money.

BERNICE: Fine. Have it your way. We're told not to be pushy.

CLAUDE: And doing pretty well, mom.

BERNICE: Thank you, son.

(a beat)

BERNICE: Which brings me to my point. There's something I need done.

BERT: No kidding!

BERNICE: Oh dear. Am I being pushy, already?

CLAUDE: No, no... Traditionally, when the dead return? It is in order to accomplish something. It's, well, inevitable!

BERNICE: Good. I'm inevitable. I like that.
(BERNICE parades back and forth.)
Okay then, this is it. Here is the scoop. Someone got it all foxed. I DO NOT, I repeat, DO NOT, want to wear this cream colored dress!. I don't know who told them that. Probably that Jackie.

FIFI: yips

BERNICE: She just doesn't think. By the time they have me all pumped up with that embalming fluid, when you put me in this cream-colored outfit of mine, why I just look like death warmed over. And besides, from what I can make out already, everybody and their favorite pet!

FIFI: yips

20

BERNICE: ...is in cream up there this year. It just looks like an ocean of dead office managers. Just a sea of them. And I want something a little different!
       (a beat)
So I went right up to the Big Guy. You'd be proud of me, boys.
       (BERNICE smiles.)
And I said...
       (BERNICE stage front)
"I don't think I can stand to wear my cream outfit for an eternity up here." And do you know what He said? Boys? He said,
       (BERNICE spreads arms looking up)
"GOD HELPS THOSE WHO HELP THEMSELVES."
       (a beat)
Took the words right out of my mouth!
So I got right to work and started pulling some strings. And well, here I am...
       (BERNICE curtsies.)
...boys.

CLAUDE: That's great, mom.

BERT: Yeah.

CLAUDE: Really cool.

BERNICE:: But enough of that. Here is what I want you to do. Bert!
       (somewhere in this speech BERNICE will pace back and forth, stage front,
         like Patton)
You tell that Jackie flatly, "THE CREAM WON'T DO." And Claude.
       (CLAUDE is dazzled.)
Wake up! And then find out where they've stored my old red satin gown and my stilhetto heels!... my 'happy hooker' slings. I intend to shake things up a little, here. And I would like the fox stole, and GOOD nylons. I don't know how things will wear up there. And if either of you wanted to stuff a bouquet or two of flowers left over from the funeral service into the coffin beside me, I wouldn't mind that.
       (a beat)
I didn't go to all the trouble of dying just to become a burden on my relations. But, on the other hand, (regards her situation), sometimes presentation IS everything! So remember that. And I don't intend to look like Hell! for all Eternity.
       (Electrical discharges. Smoke.)
And, I guess, that's it.

       (Fog clears. BERNICE is gone.) (The corpse remains.)

(Spotlight is on...)

CLAUDE: (in shock)

BERT: (in shock also)

END OF ACT ONE

ACT TWO

SETTING: The funeral parlor that same day. JACKIE is on a small step arranging lilies around the casket, when CLAUDE (carrying a box of his mother's clothes) and BERT enter. BERT walks to the coffin.

BERT: Jackie?

FIFI: panting

JACKIE: Look! who I found crammed into Bernice's coffin.
        (JACKIE steps regally forward with FIFI.)
And I found her with this!
        (Displays empty whiskey bottle.)

FIFI: (hiccups.)

BERT: (peering into coffin) Honey? You know that I don't want you angry. But I've told you time and again! "The cream won't do!"

JACKIE: (mounting step) And I've told you time and again Bertie, don't worry your little head about it.

BERT: Jackie. It is VERY IMPORTANT that my mother NOT be buried in her cream suit.

CLAUDE: (nods)

JACKIE: (looking down, exasperated) Oh Bert. Why?

       (We hear a rumble.)

BERT: (glances upwards) Because everybody up there is wearing cream, for Godsakes!

JACKIE: What?

BERT: ...And it's such a little thing. We just exchange a little of this, for a little of that.

CLAUDE: (holding carton) We have the items.

> (JACKIE inspects items in cardboard box, including good   nylons, red dress and happy hooker heels.)

JACKIE: Claude? You share Bert's perversions? Tell me you aren't possessed by the same demons?

CLAUDE: They're our inheritance.

JACKIE: This whole family is sick!

BERT: But we can fix it! We have the opportunity now! honey, to put to rest what has oppressed us, beaten us down, belittled us and beleaguered us...

CLAUDE (holding up box) Indeed, yes! We can bury the ghost of our past. All it asks... is that we outfit it properly!

BERT: It's our one chance.

CLAUDE: And I really think it's a good idea, too!

JACKIE: Claude... it's always a wonder what you think.
> (a beat)

Bert. Let's retrace our steps: I said, "I'm tired of hearing you say unkind things about your mother, AND women in general." Whether or not they were true, Fifi and I didn't care. But we were getting tired of hearing it. After a while, it was just ...tiresome. And so, we made deal - for your very soul, it seems! (indicating the carton) Everytime your mother was mentioned, you would say something nice about her, something sweet. And in return, Fifi and I would oversee all aspects of your mother's funeral in an efficient, and thrifty manner, including cooking for the wake, calling relatives, ordering the flowers and what not...."

BERT: I know, honey. I know...

JACKIE: In other words, I'M IN CHARGE.
> (a beat)

Because you were in deep DENIAL, honey. You wanted nothing to do with your mom's passing. Your mom's death! "I just want it all to go away." Those were your exact words, am I right?

BERT: You're right, honey. You're right. But NOW, she will!

CLAUDE: (aping BERT) We've as good as got mom's word!

JACKIE: And I filled in for you, Bertie. Because I realized that this was the first stage of your grief. That you were just beginning the grieving process honey. You're so unconscious! anyway.
  (a beat)
And look how STILL Bernice is, for once.
  (sighs)
It's sad in a way. ...It's like you're missing it all. It's like you're missing it all!

BERT: Sweetie? Honey? Would you JUST take mom OUT of that beige, and put her INTO the red satin?

JACKIE: (standing regally) And I say NO.
  (a beat)
There comes a time in every married woman's life when the crown is passed. The Queen is dead! (turning) Long live the Queen!

BERT: (to CLAUDE) What does that mean?

CLAUDE: It bodes ill, I'm thinking.

JACKIE: The Death of the Queen! With these creamy lilies showcasing that dress! the color of mother's milk... pure and unadulterated. Before which all of the surviving remnants of her matriarchy gather to witness the passing of power...
  (a beat)
Versus dressing up your dead mother to look like a slut.

  (JACKIE shakes her head, purses her lips in a silent, "no", and taps the air
   with a lily to indicate the interview is over.)

  (lights out on JACKIE)

  (Sounds of FRASIER theme song. Spotlight on DR. PEHRL in his office
  as CLAUDE, pulling BERT, approaches.)

DR. PERHL: Ahh. So my practice, it is expanding!

SCENE 2

SETTING: Day TWO. BERT is in the funeral parlor pouring himself and FIFI
drinks from a whiskey bottle on top of the casket.

BERT: (toasting BERNICE's corpse) Who could have foreseen it mother?

FIFI: (yips)

BERT: And now what?

        (BERT closes FIFI in casket again with whiskey bottle.)

BERT: (squinting offstage left) Herb? ...Bottleman?

HERB: (enters, dressed for funeral)   The same.

BERT: What the hell are you doing here?

HERB: In truth, I felt that an outpouring of grief might be in order.

BERT: I am afraid that your tears are not going to move me!

HERB: Don't be! afraid. (blowing nose loudly, then wiping) It takes a man to reveal
their emotions.
        (opens casket to view BERNICE's corpse)

FIFI: (yips)

HERB: (ignores FIFI) She still looks vigorous! (studies whiskey bottle) Hasn't lost an
inch of her presence, if you ask me.
        (a beat)
So. How are you taking it?

BERT: (putting bottle away) Taking what?

HERB: (rapping on coffin) Your mother's death!
        (poking her)
She's definitely dead.

BERT: Will you sit down, and quit that...

       (HERB raises cane defensively)

BERT: ...before I wrap that thing of yours around your ears!

HERB: Sounds reasonable.
       (shuts lid on FIFI who gives a muffled yip)
       (HERB sits quickly in single chair, stage center.)
Well, then. Here I am. Herb Bottleman, your servant in grief. What can I do for you?

BERT: You could leave!

HERB: Sounds reasonable. (not moving) But there again...
       (a beat)
In truth! I feel partly responsible... And, after speaking with you, if I might speak with that Jackie! Because! as best I can, as best as I am able! I am willing to hurl myself into the breech! to make amends.
BERT: There's no need to hurl yourself anywhere Herb.
       (a beat)
Especially "the breech".

HERB: But I want to.

BERT: (malevolently) But I don't want you to.

HERB: Nevertheless, I feel the need to do something. (smiles, thinking of JACKIE) ...That there is something I need to do!

BERT: (advancing) Yes. And this is how it works. Mother is gone... and now you're going. Right?

       (HERB raises cane defensively)

CLAUDE: (enters) Herbert? Bottleman?

HERB: The same.

BERT: (wielding bottle) You seize his cane Claude, and I'll club him!

CLAUDE: (holds palm up) Bert.
      (CLAUDE, circles HERB, fixed on lone chair stage center, clockwise.)
Calm down. Because I think I can talk to...
      (inhales, centering himself)
this Herb! After all, there is a saying in the business world, isn't there, Herb, that "reasonable people always agree"?

HERB: (keeping his eye on BERT) I think it best to keep my own council, if you don't mind.

CLAUDE: Herb. Our family has just suffered a death. Do you understand what I am saying?

HERB: I certainly do. That's why I'm here!

CLAUDE: And Herb. We are ALL encumbered by our grief.

HERB: That's entirely understandable. In fact, I would go as far to say, Bernice would be pleased.

CLAUDE: (still circling) And, perhaps you can see as how we're all pretty busy, even Jackie!

HERB: That is why I am here! To offer my services.

CLAUDE: Jackie doesn't need your services!

HERB: What? She has been talking about ME?

      (CLAUDE halts.)

BERT: (to CLAUDE) You see!

HERB: (to CLAUDE) You wouldn't know where my "Jacqueline" might be, would you? Perhaps you could tell me what she has been saying?

BERT: She hasn't been saying anything!

HERB: (with concern to CLAUDE) She's alright, isn't she?

      (BERT and CLAUDE look at each other.)

HERB: This is where she's most likely to show up, isn't it? She wouldn't have gone somewhere, would she?

BERT: Jackie is not going anywhere!

HERB : (troubled look to CLAUDE) He certainly sounds certain.

CLAUDE: (circling counterclockwise) Herb! How is it a person comes by an outlook such as yours?

HERB: What outlook? All I'm saying is, my Jackie looks good!

CLAUDE: And especially now. Where our mother lies dead! Don't you feel bad about saying such things?

HERB: Quite the contrary. Declaring my affections makes me feel like a Man! Like a King! You boys should both try it.

BERT: Herb…We have no affections for you.

HERB: (looks at CLAUDE)

CLAUDE: (shakes his head)

HERB: Surely, there's someone you like.

        (a beat)

CLAUDE: Herbert! What I am saying is, that if I were in your situation I would feel that attending the funeral of a departed older woman friend - who apparently had feelings for me, and I helped kill! - in order to run away with the more attractive wife! of her eldest son would be, well... nearly unforgivable!

HERB: There's! a hurdle for you.

CLAUDE: But what I have the MOST trouble with is your seemingly completely amoral world outlook.

HERB: Oh! It's no trouble.

CLAUDE: You're like a reptile!

HERB: I couldn't feel more warm blooded.

CLAUDE: It's like you haven't a care in the world!

HERB: That's how I feel! Now we're getting somewhere! So. You haven't seen my Jackie, have you?

BERT: (by coffin) YOUR Jackie? (to CLAUDE) Let's kill him! That's what I say! And stuff him in here with mom! That would be fitting.

HERB: (retreats offstage) Violence is never the answer.

BERT: It works for me! Let's do away with him! It can be as simple as that!

HERB: (peeking out a door, HERB blows a raspberry) Nya, nya!

　　　　(BERT runs after HERB)

CLAUDE: Why does everybody come on so selfishly and egotistically? This is what I STILL can't understand.

FIFI: (still in coffin) yips

SCENE 3

SETTING: The funeral parlor is dark. We are THREE days in. CLAUDE is downstage left, lying on the psychiatrist's couch. DR. PERHL is seated, listening.

CLAUDE: (despairing)   Now it seems, I mean the appearance I get is that EVERYBODY is a stalker.
　　(a beat)
And I don't know how to talk to people... I can't relate... It seems I make no impact. Even with family, AND guests. I pee all over myself...

30

DR. PERHL: So. Your life, it is not working still?

CLAUDE: Nein! I mean, no! Mom is dead. And Bert is apparently well on his way to alcoholism. And his wife is starting to go goofy. All the while I have barely even gotten started! in life... Oh why does everybody come on so strong? This is what I STILL can't believe!

DR. PERHL: So. You want I should give you some advice?

CLAUDE: Ja! I mean... YES!

DR. PERHL: Well then!. You must get a new personality. This Claude... Gustafson. (shaking head) ...does not work. Not at all!

CLAUDE: What are you talking about?
          (a beat)
You mean, no more Mr. Nice Guy?

DR. PERHL: (shakes head) Nein. I mean, no more Claude! No more Mr. Claude Gustafson! ...Gone. Kaput!

CLAUDE: Huh?

DR. PERHL: Ja. What you must do? In my opinion? You must scrap this Claude!
          (a beat)
Yup. At best the most I can see is that you will make a little profit by chopping him up and selling off the more profitable aspects. But, really, what you have here is a buggy-whip.

CLAUDE: You mean, that I'm worthless?

DR. PERHL: Me? Myself? I am saying nothing. But as a professional I am forced to look at how the market is responding...
          (gesticulates sawtooth profits graph, then, profits fall)

CLAUDE: But what am I to do? I mean, can I just be somebody else?
          (a beat)
What are you suggesting? That I just up and pretend to be someone else, because what I am is a miserable failure?

DR. PERHL: Well sure!

(a beat)

And why not?

CLAUDE: But what about ME? What about my identity? Who I really am?

DR. PERHL: (pointing) You still do not get it, do you? It is your VALUES, and not your personality that make you... the wonderful person who you are! Thank God.
        (DR. PERHL imitates JOHN WAYNE)
Why a personality is just so much flash and dash there in the pan, little feller...
        (DR. PERHL back as himself.)
You see? (DR. PERHL pulls on suspenders) Is still me!
        (DR. PERHL as JOHN WAYNE)
So hang your hat on that... little pilgrim.

CLAUDE: But that's... prostitution.

DR. PERHL: (as himself) Is good acting! I think?

CLAUDE: But I don't want to be a prostitute... I mean, an actor.

DR. PERHL: How do you know? Have you tried it?

CLAUDE: But how can I be somebody else? Who could I be?

DR. PERHL: How should I know? Pick someone out. Somebody you know, and admire! (pulling on suspenders, thinking of himself) Or SOMEONE who has captured... your mother's EYE, perhaps.
        (waves finger)
Someone who has GOT what you WANT! This is America! So why not be a winner? Go for the gusto! So pursue your life, liberty, and happiness for God's sake!

CLAUDE: You're right... You're right. When you put it like that.
        (thinking of HERB)
In truth! I can see that you're right.

DR. PERHL: So go now! Give them hell, hit the groundt runnink, and all that...

CLAUDE (trying out walking like HERB) Indeed, there's no time like the present!

DR. PERHL: So Go. ...Go!

CLAUDE: (Shuffling slow, bent and wobbling like HERB) Even at my age!

DR. PERHL: (seeing him out)

> (CLAUDE shuffles off stage right, as BERT and JACKIE enter arguing, stage left.)

BERT: I can't believe I'm back here.

JACKIE: And I can't believe you would be willing to go into therapy with your brother, when you hadn't even considered! the possibility! of entering counseling with your wife. Why, it's... perverse!

> (DR. PERHL offers JACKIE a box a tissues as she marches in.)

FIFI: yips

JACKIE: (hugging dog) And Fifi thinks so, too.

DR. PERHL: And So. Tell me please. What is the problem, today?

BERT: (sighs) The problem is, was, and always... my mother.

JACKIE: Well! At least there, we agree.

FIFI: yips

BERT: And maybe that dog.

DR. PERHL: (writes like waitress taking an order) So, the mother of course. And one dog, (talking baby talk to FIFI) is another problem, eh?

BERT: Which I can take care of on my own nickel, thank you.

FIFI: whines

JACKIE: Who he shut up in the coffin, again!

FIFI: yips

JACKIE: With his dead mother.
(JACKIE talking to FIFI) Oh sweetie, what is it you feel? What is it you want?

FIFI: panting

BERT: (looking at ceiling) What do I feel? What do I want? I want all of this to be over with. I was sick of mom alive, and now, I'm sick of mom dead! But it's like she's the Rocky Mountains, and I can't get out of Denver. I mean, I'm worn out. I feel like I'm trying to bury Pike's Peak.
(Bert holds his hands up.)
For three days now!

FIFI: stops panting

　　　　(a beat)

DR. PERHL: (scratching out and correcting) So. One rotting mother ... and her dress! If I recall?

JACKIE: Her dress is just fine.

BERT: Jackie.

JACKIE: Dr. Perhl, do you see what I am up against? EVERYTHING in our marriage he blames on his mother - and then, of course, upon me! And not only that, but then he says that she speaks to him? and says that she wants to be buried in her red dress?

DR.PERHL: Umm. (puffs pipe)

BERT: (counting on his fingers) With her fox stole. New nylons.

JACKIE: And happy hooker slings!

DR. PERHL: Umm! And you are worried! That maybe you are married to some kind of a sexual psychopath?

JACKIE: Well, yes!

DR. PERHL: Or even, (darkly) a dog murderer?

FIFI: yips

　　　　(JACKIE with horror, holds FIFI tighter.)

BERT: Now wait a minute!

DR. PERHL: And that he might tie you down with strips of the torn dress WHICH he maintains is for the burial of his dear sweet angel of a mother... And perhaps while you are naked! and writhing already on the bed! paralyzed mit ze fear...

FIFI: (pants, and will pant harder with the rising sexual excitement)

JACKIE: (tugging at tissues) I think it could happen...

DR. PERHL: That he might have his way with you?

JACKIE: (breathing hard) Yes, yes...

BERT: Let's just hold it!

JACKIE: Oh yes, yes, yes, yes....

DR. PERHL: ...all the while dreaming that you are his MOTHER?

JACKIE: (in tears) ...yessss!

FIFI: (climaxes sexually)

DR.PERHL: No. I don't think so.

FIFI: (sighs)

BERT: (sighs) Thank you Dr. Charlatan.

JACKIE: Why not?!

DR. PERHL: Because he imagines his mother here, you see?

BERT: But she IS here. She IS here, I tell you.

JACKIE: And I'm telling you that your mother is dead, Bert. Dead!

DR. PERHL: Perhaps it is this way, perhaps it is that. But you see! In his soul, our dear Mr. Moneybags is still a good boy!

JACKIE: (to BERT) Is that true?

BERT: No, it's not. It's not true, honey. My soul is dark! Corrupted by money.

Honest it is.

DR. PERHL: And so, would not dare so such sexual! things while his dear mother is still around.

BERT: And she's not my "dear" mother.

JACKIE: (losing hope) Oh Bert.

BERT: And I still can't believe I'm paying for this!

DR. PERHL: But you are! you see. (to JACKIE) And so! Perhaps next session, the two brothers might like to delve into the symbology of dresses? and of their many varied meanings in dreams ...and otherwise?

BERT: Are you kidding?

JACKIE: (blowng nose loudly and waving her hand) I think you and Claude should go.

SCENE 4

SETTING: Empty funeral parlor. Funeral music. We hear HERB's shuffle and clump of his cane, as HERB cautiously sticks his head in. Seeing that all is clear, HERB settles himself alone on one of two chairs center stage, looking into the air while practicing what he has written on a scrap of paper.

HERB: (writing) Let's see. "Jackie. To My Dearest Lovemuffin". No. That sounds like I think she's chubby. How about, "To My Major Babe"? ...It's contemporary.

(As music fades, a depressed and distracted BERNICE enters.)

(HERB adjusts his hearing aid and notices angel BERNICE)

HERB: Holy poopscoops! Bernice!

(BERNICE exhausted, sinks into chair.)

BERNICE: Shut up, Herb. I've no time for pleasantries and buttery words now.

HERB: (anxious) What's the rush?

BERNICE: (sighs) I'm very busy. I'm on my way to my eternal resting place.

HERB: That's good, Bernice. You resting..

     (HERB and BERNICE are sitting stage front, reminiscent of how they sat
        on the sofa in Act 1, with HERB looking at angel BERNICE looking
        glumly back at him.)

HERB: Well. Imagine this.

BERNICE: (looking around too) Yes. Just imagine this! It's been FOUR DAYS! I go
to all the trouble to get back to Earth. Still in beige! And my two sons run off. Now
where are they?

HERB: Overcome by their grief, I suppose?

BERNICE: I can just imagine. (shaking her head) It's just like when they were boys.
And they'd been up to something, and they'd thought I couldn't sniff it out. But I did!
Just as I've sniffed out something now.

HERB: (holding up palms) Bernice, I ... (worried) What have you sniffed out?

BERNICE: That they're not going to do as I told them!
     (a beat)
Oh Herb, I'm starting to rot! Could I have a hug?

HERB: You?! A hug?
     (Walks reluctantly towards coffin.)

BERNICE: Not THAT Bernice, Herb. THIS Bernice.

     (HERB hugs BERNICE, very carefully.)

BERNICE: (glumly) My boys never hug me.

HERB: That's nice. (unfolding scrap of paper) Say Bernice. Have you got time to hear a little er ...well, doggerel?

BERNICE: (pulled from her glum thoughts) A little... what?

HERB: A poem! (unfolding it)

BERNICE: Oh Herb.. What with all of this - my death! and all - and you want me to take time out to listen to... poetry?

HERB: Now, it's not as bad as all that! Bernice. You're here! And. Well. That's partly what I want to find out. You know, if it's compelling?

BERNICE: Oh. Well, I suppose. (Collecting herself to listen.) What's it about?

HERB: Love!

BERNICE: Love?

HERB: Love!!

BERNICE: Oh... Oh, well!! (moving closer) Love!! And what is its title?

HERB: Mind you, this is just a working title.

BERNICE: (patting him on the leg) That's perfectly alright Herb. I even know what that's called, thanks to my son Claude. (moving closer) It's called, (nods proudly) "a work in progress".

HERB: That's it exactly! That's precisely what I am up to.
          (a beat)
Are you ready to hear my poem?

BERNICE: Herbie, sweets. I am all ears. You have my undivided attention.

          (BERNICE will primp at the bits of herself she believes HERB is referring
          to.)

HERB: "Herbert J. Bottleman's Love Epistle"

BERNICE: (smiles.)

HERB: Your eyes twinkle like stars. / Your teeth shine like moons. / Your thighs are like vanilla dunes.
>(BERNICE unsettled)
Your breasts are like coconut macaroons.
>(BERNICE completely flustered)
>(HERB folds paper, finishes)
In short, I swoon.
>(a beat)
So. What do you think?

BERNICE: Herb. (embarassed) Why that's wonderful!

HERB: Really? You think so? Because it's the first such thing I've ever written.

BERNICE: You have won me over!

HERB: (leaning away) ...Really?

BERNICE: (patting his hand) Yes. But I have a confession of my own to make.

HERB: Oh Bernice, there's no need to get back on that horse again.

BERNICE: I'm married.

HERB: Oh? Bernice, you're a closer! (looking at casket) And just when we all thought you were down-for-the-count. You move fast!

BERNICE: (shy) Thank you Herb.

HERB: So where is he? Where is the lucky fellow?

BERNICE: (embarassed) Well. He isn't here right now. You see ...I was PREVIOUSLY married.

HERB: And you had some nice kids out of it, too! Though the one IS... a little autistic.

BERNICE: That's artistic, Herb. And I know what you mean.

HERB: He may still grow out of it.

BERNICE: We can hope. But what I have to tell you Herb is this.

HERB: Yes?

BERNICE: (pats HERB's hand) I still love my husband.

HERB: No kidding.

BERNICE: (excited) And he's here! Herb.

HERB: (glancing about cautiously) But, you said...?

BERNICE: Just not presently.

(HERB relaxes.)

BERNICE: And I hadn't in the least! expected it myself. Which just goes to show, that you never know. But I can just see him through the gates.

HERB: (looking upwards in direction BERNICE is gesturing) No kidding.

BERNICE: But the problem is, that everywhere he goes, he is just SURROUNDED, by this crowd of younger women.
(breaking down)
Oh I suppose he thinks he's in heaven! I tell you Herb, if I had known that this would be my eventual reward for living to a ripe old age, I would have done away with myself long ago! (showing fists) While I still had a fighting chance!

HERB: Oh Bernice. "Sometimes a man cherishes the wisdom an older woman brings to a relationship. " I don't see anything in all of this yet, to be despondent about.

BERNICE: (perking up) Herb. That's my thinking, EXACTLY! My goodness, you have an understanding of women.
(thinks a minute, bats eyes)
Which brings me to my problem.

HERB: (leans further back) Eh?...

BERNICE: When Bob and I first met, I wore this ravishing outfit! Why it just mesmerized him, let me tell you that! And I have a sneaking hunch... I don't know why, but I just have this sneaking hunch, that if I can just get myself outfitted in the very same way as when we first met! well... That I can STILL bring this off!

HERB: Go get him Bernice!

BERNICE: Which is why I could use your help.

HERB: Anything.

BERNICE: I want you to talk to Jackie.

HERB: Excellent!

BERNICE: And tell her that, "the CREAM WON'T DO!" She has absconded with my red dress, stiletto heels, pearls, fox stole... Why ALL of my clothes seem to be missing! And I just can't seem to get through to her. And, I couldn't help noticing, that she seemed to warm to you...

HERB: (leaning forward) You really think so...?!

BERNICE: If you can call me, or my son, that Bert! ...any judge.

HERB: (rising to run off) You scratch my back Bernice, and I'll scratch yours!

BERNICE: (helping HERB to rise) We've no time for THAT now, Herb.

HERB: (up and tottering) Just a figure of speech Bernice. But...
        (a beat)
You don't know where that Jackie might BE, do you?

BERNICE: Yes I do, Herb. She is in the funeral home sales offices right now! mulling over the cheese samples for the wake.

HERB: Then I'd better hustle. (HERB leaves at his quickest. Waves.) Nice seeing you! kid.

BERNICE: (waving) Goodbye! Herb. Tell her I like Stilton!

SCENE 5

SETTING: DR. PERHL's office, downstage left. BERT and CLAUDE (with cane)   are there sitting in the midst of shoes, cartons leaking undergarments and a rack of BERNICE's dresses.

DR. PERHL: (who is lifting and displaying a girdle) So our meetings take a curious turn.

     (BERT and CLAUDE look fairly glum.)

CLAUDE: (as HERB) Dr. Perhl, could I say something?

DR. PERHL: Certainly.

CLAUDE: I think that perhaps you are making a theoretical error in linking Bert's fixation with the death of his mother... ...to a fetish symbol such as the red dress, when he had never actually seen our mother in the red dress during her lifetime.

BERT: Thank you baby brother.

CLAUDE: Isn't it true that fetishes are most likely the result of received experience? And that for the fetish to grow and thrive, especially a sexual one...

DR. PERHL: I would remind you, that nearly all fetishes are sexual! In fact, ven I dink about it. . .

BERT: Please don't 'dink' about it.

DR. PERHL: Most of it, everything it is sexual.
     (finds the red party dress)
Ah! And here it is. The specimen of concern, and perhaps unbridled passion?

CLAUDE: (cold to it) But my point is, that if a fetish most likely takes root it's during those years of most heightened sexual response in the male - that is, Bert's teen years. And he was a Young Republican.

BERT: And now I'm an Old Withered Republican, I suppose. So what is your point?

CLAUDE: I don't understand the causality.

BERT: Well I'm just sick of everyone blaming Republicans for everything. When our whole culture is out of round, reeling! in fact. And mothers are dropping from ceilings. Good government can't fix everything.

DR. PERHL: I agree. But tell me... does this particular dress do anything for you, either?

CLAUDE: (sadly) Just like the others. I can't say it moves me in any way.

BERT: I am as cold as ice.

DR. PERHL: So. We have been all through your mother's old dresses, ja?

BERT: Ja. Und nylons and undergarments too.

DR. PERHL: Without a hint of evidence of passion.

BERT: Boy that's it in a nutshell. You have buttonholed that one. Now maybe if you could give me a note to Jackie, so I could resume my marriage, we could get on with our lives?

CLAUDE: Awk!
          (This is the closest I can get to the open throated groaning sound
          old geezers make, when they get excited, or are undergoing
          great strain. HERB does this too.)
I get it!

BERT: Claude, I have to hand it to you. You're always the first across the finish line when there's nothing to get.

CLAUDE: It's not our fetish you are investigating. It's our lack of fetish!

DR. PERHL: Ah my Claude. You are always the most perceptive.

BERT: I know what this is. This is one of those games where there are no right answers. And you never get done. You never leave. And you never go home to your wife and children.

CLAUDE: Bert, you have no children.

BERT: Yes, well neither do you!

CLAUDE: (to DR. PERHL) Do you think that's pertinent?

DR. PERHL: What is for me to say? What I feel, my poor Claude, is that we have a curious disconnection between two boys and their poor mother, who is circling in the air trying to inhabit a certain dress for reasons that are as yet unapparent to me.
But if you were to ask me, do I think you want to sleep with your mother? I would have to say no. In fact, it seems that her very presence bothers you.

BERT: That's it! A clean bill of health! And if you'll just write that down doctor, we're out of here.

SCENE 6

SETTING: Funeral parlor, the FIFTH DAY. JACKIE is shaking her head as she culls the worst of the dead lilies and hangs air fresheners.

JACKIE: (breathes whiff of BERNICE and shuts the coffin lid) Would you hand me another air freshener please, Sir Herbie?

BERT: (running in waving his receipt, halts) Sir Herbie?

      (HERB shuffles into motion from his position as a Royal Guard of the
         air freshener carton.)

HERB: Certainly, my precious Queen.

BERT: Precious Queen?

HERB: I worship her.

JACKIE: He worships me.

BERT: Maybe he's had a stroke?

JACKIE: He claims the sun and moon rise with me.

BERT: Ask him if he knows his name? Make him count to ten?

HERB: I would kiss the ground my 'Jackie' stands upon! One, two, three, four, five, six, seven, eight, nine, ten! times. If I could get back up.

JACKIE: His mental state seems just fine.

HERB: She is so glorious and imposing. To prostrate myself would be sublime!

JACKIE: And he wants us to make love!

BERT: I think I'm going mad.
          (HERB makes sure he's in front of BERT)

HERB: First in line, cupcake! (waving air freshener) And here's my ticket.

BERT: (tossing his receipt) And here's mine, too, Jackie. But making love in a funeral parlor, where my mother is rotting... spoils the mood!

HERB: (moving towards JACKIE) The boy is too prissy. Too many delicate scruples is how I'd put it.
          (hands JACKIE an air freshener)

JACKIE: Oh Herbie, how is it you are always there for me?
          (receives air freshener)
When my husband is not.
          (kisses HERB on the cheek)

HERB: (to BERT) You see!

BERT: I AM mad.

JACKIE: Honestly, it makes me wonder why I should spend even one more second with you.
          (a beat)
What is it? What does your Inner Soul need, Bert?

BERT: What my Inner Soul NEEDS Jackie, and I've been TRYING to tell you (thrashing his arms) - in several different body languages - is a little PEACE!

JACKIE: It doesn't want ME?

BERT: Maybe it would! If you had the sense of a RABBIT?

JACKIE: (tossing down air freshner) That does it. I don't have to take that!

      (JACKIE grabs FIFI)

FIFI: Yip

      (HERB grabs JACKIE's hand.)

HERB: Time to scoot! peaches.

BERT: (following after) He's barely got brainstem activity, honey. What are you doing?

JACKIE: After all this? (hugging FIFI) WE're leaving! For Palm Beach.

FIFI: yips excitedly

HERB: (leading the way) That's right! cupcake. Sunny beaches! where the sun glosses the glistening bodies like butter as they breed.

FIFI: pants

      (HERB and JACKIE (with FIFI) are retreating, when HERB runs into CLAUDE entering with his receipt.)

      (Music from "The Good, Bad, and the Ugly begins.)

      (HERB and CLAUDE scrutinize each other, as if staring vaguely into a mirror.)

CLAUDE: (as HERB as JOHN WAYNE) Hold it right there, Pilgrim.

HERB: (squinting) Have we met?
(to JACKIE) He reminds me of someone.

JACKIE: This is Claude! Bert's younger brother.

HERB: (recoils) Seems to have aged. And he sounds like... John Wayne?

CLAUDE: (as HERB) Well, I feel better than I have in years!

HERB: You look worse. And that's no joke. Better check what you've been eating son. Lots of roughage, that's what I'd recommend. You look sort of, bound up.

CLAUDE: Could be the weight of wisdom. (Harumph) Yes, it's the burden of consciousness, I think. (wiggles pelvis) Kind of makes me "fluctuate!" you know?

HERB: Whatever it is? Best to poop it out!

JACKIE: (hiding behind HERB) They're BOTH crazed with grief, I think.

HERB: (confiding with JACKIE) Grief can play strange tricks, that's for sure!

JACKIE: But I'm afraid it's more than that, Herb. I can no longer anticipate what they will do!

HERB: (taking JACKIE's hand, and eyeing CLAUDE and BERT) Fear is a natural response. Maybe we should trust it.

CLAUDE: On the other hand, we should not to be ruled by it.

HERB: (stepping forward) Maybe you should.

CLAUDE (meeting the challenge) I think not.

        (CLAUDE stares HERB down.)

CLAUDE: I challenge you to a battle of personas.

        (HERB and CLAUDE cross canes as if in a sword fight.)

        (SWORD fight begins!)

HERB: (gaining the upper hand) You're BERNICE's son, aren't you? The autistic one.

CLAUDE: (pressing back) That's artistic!

        (CLAUDE recovers, his cane rising against HERB's pressure.)

CLAUDE: Yes, more and more, I think so.
        (advancing, one arm akimbo) (Fight continues!)

CLAUDE: And you're Herbert Bottlemen, aren't you? The man who intends to steal "that Jackie!"

>(THEIR canes clash again!)

BERT: Yeah!

JACKIE: Oh fight for me Bert! Are you going to fight for me?

BERT: As soon as I can find a cane!

HERB: (backed into JACKIE) And I think... time to scoot, honey! They're looney!

JACKIE: Oh, I think you're right!

HERB: (backpedalling against CLAUDE's ferocious onslaught) This fellow here especially. He spooks! me. Best to run for our lives!

>(HERB grabs JACKIE's hand, toddles off.)

>(CLAUDE waves his cane and chases HERB out - both moving at a
>snail's pace - with BERT backed up behind.)

CLAUDE: (toddling after) You psycho... sexual... gerontolopath!

>(CLAUDE exits.)

BERT: (watching, depressed) Claude? ...Jackie?

>(Deserted, BERT contemplates strangling his dead mother.)

BERT: Rest in peace, huh?

>(As BERT is strangling the dead BERNICE, violently! the live BERNICE
>descends.)

BERNICE: Bert? Son?

BERT: ?

BERNICE: What are you doing?

(BERT habitual jerks to attention.)

BERT: (quickly adjusting corpse with a grunt) I'm going to be up front with you and admit right now mom, that I haven't gotten everything done that you requested.
(Pulling at corpses clothes.)
But I am going to get this snafu with your wardrobe straightened out, pronto. Claude and I have made some real progress in therapy.
BERNICE: Therapy? Well I hope it's not on my account. Because I have to say, I think I feel better than I have in years! And there is my Herb! Leaving to have a talk with that Jackie! And Claude too! THEY'll have things patched up in no time.
(a beat)
So come here son, and give your mother a hug.

BERT: (still struggling) Just a second! mom.

BERNICE: Because I think I can finally say, I. feel finally like everything in my life is handled. That I've cut a straight course for The Wild, Blue Yonder! And now, the realization has come upon me that I miss my sons. That I dearly love my two sons.
(a beat)
So hug me now Bert. Before I'm gone forever!

BERT: Mom, please!

BERNICE: Besides, you needn't worry about that silly outfit. I have gotten my Herb to handle all of that.

(We hear a rip, as BERT tears off a beige sleeve.)

BERT: You sent that Herb! after MY Jackie?

BERNICE: The same.

BERT: I swear mom, since you've died, it's like you've lost all your marbles!

BERNICE: (giddy) I guess I have! But couldn't you go a little mad! too? (opening her arms) My little precious!

BERT: You sent your KILLER, after my Jackie?

BERNICE: Oh pooh! Bert. When the chips were down, I just didn't believe you had it in you.

BERT: You're probably right. I've killed no one! I've stolen no one's wife. I don't need a cane!

BERNICE: Oh son, I just didn't believe that you could stand up to that Jackie.
        (a beat)
Whereas my Herb is a man! who can get the job done. And you watch. My Herbie! will get me outfitted to the nines.

BERT: My Herbie?

BERNICE: And not only that! But he'll have that Jackie, smiling to boot. So now, for the last time Bert... hug your mother.

BERT: (waving sleeve) Are you kidding?

BERNICE: Son. Don't you know that whatever you've thought, or whatever you've done, you are never removed from a mother's love?

BERT: Boy, that's the truth!

BERNICE: (spreading arms) Because a mother's love is Eternal. It is Non-Judgemental, it is Life! and AFFIRMING. It is Warming and Nurturing...
        (stage front to regale audience like a prophet)
It Knows all! and Sees all! And makes ALL seem possible... In a Mother's Love lies the End and the Beginning... the Alpha and Omega... It is Grand!
...and yet modest and self-effacing. Without a hint of pride, or a thought for itself or self-betterment.

BERT: That's the way I'd always IMAGINED it.

BERNICE: "A mother's love is a boy's inheritance." The American Legion says that. So you've got to stop this feeling sorry for yourself, this whining! Bert. And get on with life.

    (BERNICE has BERT by the neck and from behind.)

BERNICE: So hug your mother!

    (BERT claws the air, trying to get a grip on the Angel BERNICE)

50

BERT: I'm trying to mom, but I can't get a grip on you!

BERNICE: (still choking BERT) Okay Bert, my son. But I'm telling you. You need to get to that place where your emotions are your friends.

(BERT stops clawing the air and turns to the corpse.)

BERT: (tossing clothes) That's it. I'm burying you, in your underwear!

SCENE 7

SETTING: At the funeral service, finally, SIX days in. Dirge plays. Air fresheners are everywhere. JACKIE and HERB are conspicuously missing. BERT is wearing a neck brace. And CLAUDE is using a cane.

BERT: (coughs from the lectern behind the coffin.) Ahem.

(BERT gestures and pauses.)

(Music stops.)

(BERT strokes his neck, and resumes.)

Mom always said that, "There's people who talk, and there's people who do." So. Without anymore aDO, I say... let's plant her!

(BERNICE descends! wearing an underwear Teddy with large red flowers like polka dots.)

BERNICE: Alright. Hold it. HOLD EVERYTHING! It seems that if you want something done right then you've got to do it yourself.

(BERNICE strides to the podium, as BERT has moved around to grasp coffin, and freezes.)

(BERNICE clears throat, and pulls folded speech from Teddy.)

I have enjoyed my life. But I am not going to say, I'm going to miss it.

(CLAUDE waves his hand in front of others, and realizes he is the only one who sees BERNICE.)

BERNICE: What's over is over, and what's done is done! This is a truth that I have tried to drum into my children's heads on as many occasions as I have had a chance to. There is nothing to be gained by shedding tears and wringing our hands. Or trying to replace the cow once the gate has been left open and then shut... or whatever.
The thing is! to plunge on and to go wherever the currents of life carry you. (Spreads arms.) Which is what I've said - or tried to say till I'm blue in the face- all along!
All the while my children - or at least one of them -

(BERNICE points to CLAUDE.)

(CLAUDE looks around with embarrassment and chagrin.)

BERNICE: ...has maintained just as ardently that if we do not dig around in all the garbage and debris of our past, and air all of our dirty linen for the whole world to sniff... then we will be forced to relive these events over and over in a more mysterious and veiled form until the very end of time! And what the hell does my son Claude think he knows about eternity is what I would like to know? Being as he has lived only half as long as myself alone, and never raised teenagers. So...
        (a beat)
To all of that I say hogwash! (wipes a tear.) And... I'm going to miss myself.
        (walks to where she intends to ascend from)
But finally! If I were to offer any advice about life from the perspective of eighty-five years, and my recent demise, I would have to say, get it established, exactly how you want everything handled! That it's very hard to get your message across afterwards... especially regarding burial arrangements. Get it written down, and stipulated in the will! if you have to.

BERT (lifting coffin, shouts over rising funeral music) On three! A one...

BERNICE: Exactly how you want to be outfitted!

BERT: A two...

BERNICE: So that you don't get the run around!

BERT: And a three!

      (BERT and CLAUDE, one-handed with cane, and OTHERS lift coffin.)

BERNICE: (as she starts to fly away) Cut them off without a nickel!

      (BERNICE rises towards heaven, only to fall with a
      thump.)

BERNICE: ...if it comes to that.

CLAUDE: (leaves coffin) Here mom. Give me your foot!

      (CLAUDE shuffling forward with cane to give BERNICE a launch.)

BERNICE: Oh Claude, you little fool!

      (BERNICE is launched, but can't hold her altitude, and swings wildly, out over
      the audience.)

BERNICE: WOOOOOOOOOOO...!

                    (Black out.)

ACT THREE

SCENE I

SETTING: Back in the GUSTAFSON den, days later. BERNICE is sitting on one end of psychiatric couch disconsolate in underwear with her tiny wings and god-awful hair from having been slept on wrong, and with one of BERT'S moth-eaten, old army blankets wrapped around her. BERT is in his overstuffed chair with a wet towel over his face.

BERT: (lifting towel) Looks like you missed your flight.

BERNICE: Oh, this is such a hash!

BERT: Well. What do we do now?

BERNICE: How should I know?

BERT: I did my part.

BERNICE: You did NOT do your part.

BERT: You're in the ground, aren't you? You're planted!

BERNICE: In my underwear. For eternity! I just can't believe my own son would let me down so. It just makes me sick.

(CLAUDE enters dressed like HERB, with cane.)

CLAUDE: In truth, I still miss you mom.

BERNICE: And Claude. What has gotten into you?

CLAUDE: I think it's the need to be positive, to see the humor of this situation.

BERNICE: There IS no humor to this situation.

CLAUDE: There you have it!

54

(CLAUDE shuffles around in circle mimicking HERB)
In truth! You've hit the nail on the head again!

(a beat)

BERNICE: (steaming) Oh, that Herb! Bottleman.

CLAUDE: Want to hear a couple good ones about the crippled and the elderly?

BERNICE: NO! And I am ashamed of you, to think I would. After the way I raised you...

(A cough. Enter DR. PERHL carrying black medical bag.)

CLAUDE: (whirling) Dr. Perhl! You came.

DR. PERHL: Of course! (taps BERNICE) Move over there Bag Lady.
(sits.)
Boy, oh boy. Vat haf ve got here?

BERNICE: (gruffly near tears) What we have here... is a soul in torment!

DR. PERHL: (nods)

BERNICE: And! a WOMAN... discounted. (sulky) ...whose own sons! do not love her.

BERT: Oh we do too!

BERNICE: (sulky) Do not.

BERT: Do too! Why else would we put up with you?

CLAUDE: (stomps cane) In truth... Yeah!

DR.PERHL: Children. Children.

BERT: We give you affection.

BERNICE: You buried me in my underwear!

BERT: I was upset! My Jackie is in Miami! with that Herb!

(wincing with neck pain)
And you see this THING around my neck?

DR. PERHL: (sighs) Perhaps I should have a look.

(BERT readies himself.)

(DR. PERHL opens medical bag, and pulls out tools, but examines
BERNICE instead. He looks in her mouth, eyes, etc. ...finally examining
the attachment of her tiny wings. Then puts tools away, shaking
head   sadly.)

DR. PERHL: I am afraid I was right.

BERT: Right? Right about what?

DR. PERHL: I am afraid there is nothing that can be done about your mother.

BERNICE: That's just dandy! Because, you know? Frankly, I find myself just fine.
Perfect! in fact, just the way I am.

BERT : (rubbing neck) The more things change, the more things remain the same. It is
like you've never left us mother.

CLAUDE: (nods, clomps cane) In truth, your presence dogs you.

BERT: What good are you? You sit around here. You haunt me. You annoy the air!
And you're just a flicker, but I'm tearing my hair! You're most probably two nerve
endings locked in mortal combat. But you seem damned real, nevertheless...
         (BERT goes for a drink)
And you brought EVIL into OUR home! WHO took away my JACKIE! I don't want
a mother like you! You're dead. Go away!

BERNICE: That Herb! For the life of me. He was supposed to talk to that Jackie.;NOT
run away with her. Why is it, nobody around here can do as they're told?

BERT: Maybe if you had just let me! handle it.

BERNICE: At any rate, there is no way on earth that I would consent to go anywhere
outside of this house NOW. Let alone through those Celestial Corridors of princely
fashion and power! dressed like this. Good grief! I would never have believed I could

have been brought so low. And I can't think of a thing I've done to deserve it.

CLAUDE: Dr. Perhl. You've got to help us.

BERT: Yes!

BERNICE: But nevertheless! here I am, looking like a MUDHEN! And my big break! My big day! I was going to head up the band! ...and stride right up to your father, pretty as you please! Pretty as a picture is how I had framed it. And he'd be waiting. And I would be wearing that red dress ...
    (a beat)
Just as I had! when your father was in his uniform. That would have been heaven for me. On earth. Or up There. I really can't see what difference it makes. The point is, heaven is where your heart is.
And now all I know is, here I sit. I look like hell. With this big hair! and in my underwear!

DR. PERHL: I think you two boys need to hug, your mother!

BERT: (recoils)

    (CLAUDE circles BERNICE, ignoring DR. PERHL)

CLAUDE: You know. I have found mother, that much of life is just what we take it to be. (clomps cane) There's nothing like experience, that's for sure.

BERNICE: Yes. And I've had enough. (looking around) How in the world do you suppose I'm going to get out of here?

CLAUDE: In truth! It looks to me like you're just going to have to wait until your wings grow. (CLAUDE waves cane as he circles.) Or somebody gives you a boost. Best to remain positive! (CLAUDE clomps cane again.) ...is all I can say.

BERNICE: And I just can't! I have places to go and people to see!

    (CLAUDE circles, shaking his head.)

BERT: You always have to have things your own way, don't you? You know, I spoke to your ninety year old cousin Agnes at the funeral, and just as an afterthought I asked her what you were like as a child! And do you know what she said?

BERNICE: You mean dear, sweet cousin Agnes made it all the way, to MY funeral? Now THERE, Bert, is a person you could stand to emulate. She always had a good word to say about everybody.

BERT: She said, you were "a spoiled brat."

BERNICE: Cousin Agnes said that?

BERT: Nearly her dying words.

(BERT hands BERNICE his drink.)

BERT: Here. Dribble this through your tired haze.

BERNICE: (stiffly) No thank you.

BERT: (drinks it) Waste not, want not.

DR. PERHL: Boys. Boys! Hug your mother.

BERT: I am not budging another inch.

CLAUDE: (clomps cane) Nor I.

BERNICE: Nor I! And Bert! If I EVER hear you referring to me that way again like the way you did at the funeral - as if I were some kind of a shrub! to be planted - why I'll personally wash your mouth out with soap. I don't know who taught you to act like that, but it sure wasn't me! THAT's for sure.

DR. PERHL: Okay boys. But that is it. That is my prescriptions! That what this needs is that you should BOTH show some love for your mother. (sadly, pleading) Otherwise, how is it we can make of this situation - this world! a better place? Someone has to take a step, you know.

BERNICE: Doctor, don't you know? That children are the most SELFISH things in the world. That all they have on their minds is satisfying their own greedy little needs!

BERT: That, would be a relief.

(DR. PERHL pushes BERT)

(BERT recoils)

DR. PERHL: What is it the matter? Do you think she is going to bite you?

BERNICE: I have never bitten anyone.

BERT: Couldn't we just continue arguing?

CLAUDE: Or! What if we just continued ignoring each other?

BERNICE: And you think that I have no feelings? Why, if allowed, my feelings would overwhelm you. Why I have sentiments sharper than a whirling saw. Emotions more powerful than a speeding locomotive! And miseries and griefs that could drown tall buildings in a single deluge!
        (a beat)
All the while masquerading as a mild-mannered housewife. Oh, what a tight shoe society has wedged me into.

DR. PERHL: Why won't you two boys hug your mother?

BERT: I don't know. It... just doesn't seem NATURAL somehow, is all.

CLAUDE: Yeah.

DR. PERHL: So what is natural? That your poor mother should have to come all the way back here, and be sitting here in her underwear as an angel?

BERNICE: Yeah!

BERT: You've got me there.

CLAUDE: Me too!

DR. PERHL: Extreme situations can sometimes require extreme remedies! So hug your mother, already.

(CLAUDE drops cane, hugs BERNICE as CLAUDE.)

CLAUDE: I love you! mom.

BERNICE: (stiffly) Thank you Claude.

DR. PERHL: You know, true love is mostly simply ENDURING. Bearing up to it, mostly.

CLAUDE: You really think so?

DR. PERHL: (patting CLAUDE on the shoulder) Oh ja! While you let somebody else, love you. (to BERT) So go on. Now it is your turn.
      (DR. PERHL puts back to BERT and shoves.)

BERT: Okay!

      (BERT hugs BERNICE)

DR. PERHL: And so go on now, Mrs. Bernice. And hug your children.

      (BERNICE hugs her boys)

DR. PERHL: Why was that so bad?

      (CLAUDE and BERT shake their heads)

DR. PERHL: So, go on. ...Grip her hard, already! both of you.

      (BERT and CLAUDE both hug BERNICE.)
      (BERNICE rises.)

BERNICE: (wiping tears, blowing nose) Now, I DO feel better!

DR. PERHL: Of course.

BERT: (gazing upwards and rubbing neck) And I do too!

DR. PERHL: Of course!

CLAUDE: (trying to wedge his way into happy group) And me too!

BERT: (seeing BERNICE rise) Want another hug?

BERNICE: Sure!

CLAUDE: (distressed, as BERNICE rises) Mom! You're leaving us...

BERNICE: Yes... I think so.

(daubing eyes, blowing nose again)
Oops! Now I'm falling.

BERT: Here. Let me hug you again!

(BERT is just high enough to hug her feet.)

BERNICE: There! That DOES feel about right! (tossing away tissue, wiggling feet) Yes!
I think THAT just about does it. (rising)

CLAUDE: So long mom!

BERNICE: So long sons! (a beat) I love you!

BERT and CLAUDE: We love you, too!

(BERNICE is gone)

(DR. PERHL steps stage front.)

DR. PEHRL: And so we observe, at the end of another successful therapeutic
encounter! the patients' burdens LIFTED from off of their poor shoulders - as if carried
away on the wings of angels! and back into God's lap, like one hot potato!

CLAUDE: (waving upwards) Say hi to dad!

(Enter JACKIE. She has a pennant celebrating Key West, and both she and
FIFI look worn out.)

(ALL halt.)

BERT: Jackie!

JACKIE: Oh Bert! (a beat) The powers of the Heart are IMMENSE!

BERT: I know. ...I know!

JACKIE: I guess I just lost my head.

(BERT rushes to hug her.)

JACKIE: You're hugging me!

BERT: I'm feeling my love for you!

JACKIE: What are you doing?

BERT: (sliding down to hug JACKIE'S feet) Plus, I've been getting practice.

JACKIE: (looking down, trying to speak to him) Sweetie? I'm so sorry. Would you please take me back. Please? Please? Pretty please?

BERT: (making over JACKIE's feet) Yes, yes, yes, yes,....

JACKIE: At first, Herb was a lot of fun. But then he kept smoking those big cigars and talking to his cronies about money all the time until they were ALL fluctuating. And then, finally, it just hit me... This is Bert! when he's OLDER. And I thought to myself, 'Why not have Bert, when he's younger?'

> (a beat)

JACKIE: You may rise.

> (BERT rises.)

> (JACKIE hugs an abashed BERT.)

JACKIE: I missed you so.

> (They kiss.)

BERT: Look honey, a harvest moon.

CLAUDE: (carrying a box of BERNICE's clothes) A good time to get to the task at hand.

SCENE 2

SETTING: Half-light in the graveyard under a big harvest moon. Sounds of picks and shovels being used, as the Glenn Miller song, "Moonglow" plays. BERT and CLAUDE are shoveling imaginary dirt from a hole stage left front where BERNICE's red dress and heels have been neatly arranged.

        (CLAUDE and BERT, stage front, shovel in rhythm for a while.)

CLAUDE: (halts shovelling), You know... a small plot, meager even! and bare circumstances... this is much more like life as I know it.

BERT: Well, keep it down.

CLAUDE: Plus, I somehow see mom as different, less formidable! sort of a person now.
        (turns to audience)
And maybe... in a way... mom was right! That life is like a Play! And it's best to enjoy the thing. And then to... just barge on!

BERT: (tossing dirt) "Absence makes the heart grow fonder". There is nothing new about that. And she IS a different sort of person now.
        (BERT clomps! with shovel.)
She's dead.
        (BERT stops digging, to stand with shovel and deliver his
            monologue.)
But let me tell you, I've learned my lesson...
        (stands with shovel handle crossed over chest as if acknowledging the flag)
From now on you're going to see a kinder and gentler Bert. From now on, I understand! what Jackie has been talking about, what about all this empathy! stuff.

        (As BERT continues, CLAUDE senses something and turns stage rear...)

BERT: And that those people who have successful marriages are like any other businesspersons who have taken the time to rearrange their busy schedules and make a Commitment to Excellence.

(CLAUDE and the audience see BERNICE descend, behind, spotlighted in her sexy, short red dress, with an enormous pair of beautiful wings.)

(Closing song, "I'm in Heaven", sung by Louis Armstrong begins.)

BERT: (to CLAUDE, sotto voice) Baby brother, wake up! (turns)

(CLAUDE points to their mother BERNICE.)

(TALL, DARK, HANDSOME FIGHT OFFICER, played by the actor who played HERB, steps out to offer BERNICE his arm.)

OFFICER: Hey, Bernice! The band's playing!

(BERNICE takes his arm, waves goodbye, and shimmies offstage right.)

(BERT and CLAUDE watch, pleasantly stunned.)

CURTAIN

ABOUT THE AUTHOR

Carl Nelson spent 20 years in the Seattle theater community, during which time he wrote and produced plays, directed others, and performed whenever the talent was missing but a body still needed. Before that he did stand-up comedy. Currently he is enjoying the obscurity of Belpre, Ohio where he writes poems that mosey about.

www.ingramcontent.com/pod-product-compliance
Lightning Source LLC
Chambersburg PA
CBHW060535030426
42337CB00021B/4270